A GREAT MIRACLE HAPPENED THERE

A Chanukah Story

by Karla Kuskin

illustrated by Robert Andrew Parker

Willa Perlman Books
An Imprint of HarperCollins*Publishers*

A Great Miracle Happened There: A Chanukah Story

Text copyright © 1993 by Karla Kuskin Illustrations copyright © 1993 by Robert Andrew Parker Printed in the U.S.A.
All rights reserved. Typography by Elynn Cohen   4   5   6   7   8   9   10   ❖
Library of Congress Cataloging-in-Publication Data Kuskin, Karla. A great miracle happened there : a Chanukah
story / by Karla Kuskin ; illustrated by Robert Andrew Parker   p.   cm.   "Willa Perlman books."   Summary: On the first
night of Hanukkah, a mother tells her family and a young guest the story of the holiday's origin.   ISBN 0-06-023617-5. —
ISBN 0-06-023618-3 (lib. bdg.)   I. Hanukkah—Juvenile literature.   [I. Hanukkah.]   I. Parker, Robert Andrew, ill.
II. Title. BM695.H3K87 1993   296.4'35—dc20   92-17909   CIP   AC

For Charlotte Zolotow—
Because this is your book too—
Love, gratitude, and Hag Sameach
K. K.

For my mother and father
R. A. P.

Every night the sun sets in the trees at the end of my street. Then, as the dark moves up the block, house lights and streetlamps go slowly on. I live in the third house from the corner. If you walk by tonight, you will see the light of two bright candles burning in our menorah. This is the twenty-fifth of Kislev, and we are celebrating the first night of Chanukah.

My friend Henry, who lives across the street, has come over to watch us light the candles. Henry always has questions. He wants to know what language menorah comes from and what Kislev means. He knows that Chanukah is a Jewish holiday.

Begin with those words. Chanukah, menorah, and Kislev are Hebrew words. Hebrew is a language that Jews all around the world have spoken for thousands of years. The Old Testament of the Bible was written in Hebrew. And there is a Hebrew calendar. Kislev is one of the winter months. It comes about the same time as December.

Henry admires our menorah. It is a special candelabra—a candle holder with nine places for candles. It is used only at Chanukah. My mother and I have polished the brass until it is the color of the setting sun. "Your Chanukah candles and our Christmas lights will shine across the street at each other," Henry says.

As the sun sets in the trees, my mother and I carry the menorah into the living room. My great-grandmother brought the menorah to America when she came to live in this country.

Now I hold the match and my mother holds my hand, and together we light the middle candle. This candle is called the shammas, which means servant in Hebrew. The shammas is used to light the other candles; that is how it serves them. Tonight we light just one candle with the shammas. Chanukah lasts for eight days. Every night we will light one more candle, until on the eighth night the whole menorah is ablaze.

And when the flame jumps from one candlewick to the next and rises up in a graceful, burning arc, my mother begins to recite the prayers, and I recite them with her. There are three. First we say a special blessing for the Chanukah lights. Then there is a blessing for the miracles that happened long ago. And then we say the blessing that is said on the first night of every Jewish holiday. It is called She-Heheyanu. My father comes in. He and Henry join in on the amens.

I can see the two candle flames reflected in my mother's eyes. She has a thoughtful look. We are all very quiet waiting. Then she says that a holiday usually celebrates something that happened long ago. And she begins to tell this story.

"Long ago, in the distant, misted past, there was a king named Antiochus Epiphanes who was very powerful, but he was neither wise nor good. Antiochus ruled many lands, and one of those was the land of Israel. Jerusalem was a city in Israel then, as it is today, and the events that we celebrate at Chanukah took place in that long-ago Jerusalem and the rough countryside around it.

"Because the King ruled over many different lands, he ruled many different peoples. They dressed in different ways, spoke different languages, and followed different customs. When they prayed, they prayed to different gods. But the King did not care about the different ways and wishes of his people. He followed Greek ways, so he made laws that said that everyone he ruled must wear Greek dress, follow Greek customs, and pray in Greek temples to Greek gods. 'Do as I say, or die,' said Antiochus.

"The troops of Antiochus marched into the beautiful Temple the Jews had built in Jerusalem. They destroyed the holy scrolls and books and took the Temple's treasures. They scraped the gold from the Temple walls.

"Then they made a Greek temple of the place. 'Pray as I pray,' said Antiochus, 'or die.'

"Many people were very frightened, so they obeyed the new laws. But there were some who were willing to fight and die for their beliefs. Not far from Jerusalem, in the city of Modin, there was a Jewish priest named Mattathias. He refused to follow the King's laws. When soldiers were sent to force the people to obey, Mattathias was so angry that he killed a Jewish man who did obey the soldiers, and then he killed a soldier."

At this point my mother stops talking. She looks unhappy. Then she says,

"Even though Mattathias was angry at the terrible laws, he was wrong to kill people. Killing does not change laws; it just leads to more killing."

"Absolutely," my father says quietly. Henry and I nod.

My mother continues with the story. "After Mattathias had killed the two men, he pulled down the altar in the temple in Modin. Then he cried out that everyone who believed as he did should follow him. Of course he knew that if he did not run away, he too would be killed.

"Many people who also hated the terrible laws followed him. Women, men, and children took their cattle and left their homes to live in the rough hills outside that city.

"Mattathias and his wife took their five sons. Their names were Johanan Gaddis, Simeon Thassi, Judah Maccabee, Eleazar Avarah, and Jonathan Apphus. Simeon was the wisest son and Judah was the strongest. When Mattathias died, Judah became the leader of all the Jewish warriors in the hills. They called themselves Maccabees, after him.

"Maccabee means hammer in Hebrew, and these warriors hammered at their enemies in many battles. Their fame spread. Their lives were very hard," my mother says. "Sometimes they did not have enough food. Often they slept on the cold ground. But they were determined to win back the Temple in Jerusalem, so they fought on.

"King Antiochus knew of their strength and their successes. So he put an enormous army together to stop them. Then Judah said to his men, 'Be valiant.' That means be brave and strong. They were. And after many, many battles they took back the great Temple on Mount Moriah in Jerusalem.

"Now that should have been a most wonderful time for the Maccabees. They were returning to the place they loved most in the world after long, difficult years. But the handsome gates had been burned, rooms and altars were broken down, and there were weeds and rocks everywhere. Everything that had been neat, green, shining, and lovely was destroyed and desolate."

"What did they do?"

"They went to work building, cleaning, and making the place beautiful again. Then when the Temple was all ready, the priests blessed it and everything that was in it. All this happened on the twenty-fifth of Kislev in 164 B.C. It is called the Rededication of the Temple.

"That means that the Temple was made holy again and given back to the God of the Jews. Then those who were there lit the menorah and gave thanks and prayed. And now, more than two thousand years later, we still light the Chanukah candles and pray in the same way.

"There is also a story that when the soldiers entered the Temple court, they found eight tall spears lying on the ground where they had been hurled. They took the spears and drove them, standing straight up, into the earth. Then they lit a flame at the top of each one, making the spears look like a candelabra, like the menorah.

"As long as the Jewish people can remember, it has been very important to always have a flame burning in the temple. This is called the eternal flame. Eternal means lasting forever. In those long-ago days the menorah had seven wicks dipped in oil. But when the Maccabees looked for oil to relight the flames, they found that there was only a tiny bit they could use. Most of it had been spoiled by Antiochus's soldiers.

"There was only enough good oil left to last for a single day, so the Maccabees were very worried. They were sure the flame would go out, because they knew it would take them at least a week to get new oil. But amazingly, that tiny bit of oil lasted for eight days, and the flame kept burning. On the eighth day the good new oil was brought to the Temple.

"And that is why Chanukah menorahs have places for eight candles and the shammas. It is why we light a candle every night for eight nights beginning on the twenty-fifth of Kislev, the day of the Rededication."

As my mother stops speaking, a few flakes of snow brush the window. We are all very quiet thinking about the story. Then our dog barks, my sister wakes up from her nap, and the front doorbell rings.

My mother asks Henry if he would like to stay for dinner. He would. My father goes to get my sister, and I answer the door. My grandmother, Uncle Mort, Aunt Amy, and a few snowflakes come in.

The dining table has been dressed up for the holiday. The tablecloth and napkins are even whiter than white usually is, and the glasses sparkle with little lights from the candles. Henry and I walk around looking at our faces reflected in the knives and spoons. Next to each plate there is a dreidel and a small package.

"Those are just little things," says Grandma. "When I was a girl, people didn't give Chanukah presents at all."

Henry and I shake the packages to see if we can tell what's inside them. Henry has never seen a dreidel before. Grandma spins hers, and Henry says, "It looks like a top, with something written on the sides."

"Exactly," says Grandma. She shows us that the writing is four Hebrew letters, one on each side of the dreidel, and they stand for four words. In English those words mean A Great Miracle Happened There. Henry wants to know where "There" was.

"The land of Israel," says Aunt Amy.

"And who knows what the miracle was?" my father asks.

Henry and I smile at each other. We do. He is the guest, so I let him say, "It was that the oil lasted for eight days."

We discuss miracles. Henry and I are pretty sure we believe in them. So does Aunt Amy. She thinks that a miracle is something wonderful that people cannot explain and only God can make happen. But Uncle Mort thinks that when people cannot explain something amazing, then they call it a miracle. He believes if we all knew enough, everything could be explained scientifically. Grandma doesn't think so. She says that the older she gets, the more things she can think of that cannot be explained in scientific ways.

Mother brings in the roast chicken. I like her idea. She says it seems like a miracle to her that tonight we are celebrating something that happened over two thousand years ago and still has great meaning for us. My uncle Mort nods. "Maybe it is that combination of past history and present meaning that makes a holiday a holiday," he says.

Dinner is delicious. There are potato pancakes called latkes that have been fried in oil to remind us of the special oil. Mother has made doughnuts for dessert for the same reason.

"Please pass another one of those miraculous doughnuts," Father says. "They are so light they probably can fly." Before he takes a bite of his second, or third, he wishes everyone a Hag Sameach. I start to tell Henry that those words mean Happy Holiday in Hebrew, but he has figured that out already and wishes me the same.

The snow is falling faster against the window now, and the dog is asleep underneath my father's chair. Every night in this coming week we will recall the Maccabees and the Rededication of the Temple. Every night in this coming week we will add one more candle to the menorah and light the lights again. And every night as we watch the tallow melt and the small flames die down, we will sit remembering and wondering. Then we will talk about miracles some more.

J
296.4
Kus

Kuskin, Karla.

A great miracle
happened there.

DATE			

JUN -- 1994

LC 11/10   16x   R 9/13

BAKER & TAYLOR BOOKS